Contents

Executive Summary

Over the past several years, the United States government and law enforcement agencies have become increasingly concerned with the spread and influence of Islamic radicalization amongst U.S. citizens and naturalized American individuals. Many such individuals are taking action intended to harm Americans and American interests domestically or abroad. Evidence points to a sophisticated and evolving indoctrination campaign that targets not just Americans of Muslim faith, but the larger population. It is becoming essential to view the spread of this radicalization as a technologically advanced phenomenon that should be addressed within the context of the evolving nature of the threat. This paper presents a study on practical and realistic assessments of Islamic radicalization in the United States and offers suggestions for its mitigation. In particular, the paper will address the emergence of the Internet as the battleground of ideas with the radical version of Islam, and will offer suggestions for addressing this problem for the government and law enforcement efforts.

Introduction

To help policymakers understand and discuss the approaches to countering Islamic radicalization in the United States, the Center for Technology and National Security Policy (CTNSP) Homeland Security team is conducting a study on practical and realistic assessments of this threat and proposals to mitigate it. This paper addresses the growing and evolving threat of domestic terrorism that is advocated and perpetrated by radical Islamic ideologues. Specifically, we will review terrorist attempts on American soil and against the American population in order to offer recommendations. For the purpose of this study, only Islam-inspired terrorist activity will be reviewed; other activity related to fundamentalist Christian or activist anti-U.S. government actions will not be discussed. This paper does not attempt a discourse on the Islamic religion in general. Rather, specific ideological underpinnings that have inspired a few people to acts of terrorism for the sake of Islam will be scrutinized and reviewed.

This study is necessary for several reasons. The first and most fundamental is the fact that the nature of terrorism in the United States is changing; over the past several years, major terrorist attempts were conducted by American-born or naturalized citizens.[1]

Second, there is no longer a definite profile for an individual ready to commit terrorist acts in the name of radical Islam: "The profile is broken, [and] it's women as well as men, it's lifelong Muslims as well as converts, it's college students as well as jailbirds," according to a terrorist expert at the Georgetown University.[2]

Third, the proliferation of personal technology is making it easy—and increasingly likely—for aspiring terrorists to gather intelligence, conduct surveillance, and design and carry out a terrorist act. The most notable factor linking the latest terrorist attempts is the Internet, which also offers a plethora of information on the religious ideology and indoctrination of the latest terrorist actors and suspects. Countering this latest technological trend is a formidable task for the intelligence and law enforcement community that requires development of different approaches to tracking and monitoring potential threats.

Fourth, dealing with Islamic radicalization requires improved understanding of and familiarity with the larger Muslim community in the United States, which is diverse along ethnic, social, confessional, and geopolitical lines and does not represent a single Islamic point of view.

Lastly, a review of radicalization timelines is necessary to better understand—and continuously update—the process of personal radicalization in the name of religion in order to develop better observation and prevention techniques. "It is difficult to say whether the uptick in [terrorist] cases is because law enforcement has gotten better at

---

[1] http://www.homelandsecuritynewswire.com/noticeable-increase-number-americans-arrested-al-qaeda-related-terrorism
[2] Ibid.

catching suspects or if there are simply more to catch," according to the homeland security publication on the increase in the number of Americans arrested for al-Qaeda-related terrorism.[3]

This paper reviewed the timeline of how a suspected homegrown terrorist moves quickly from adopting extremist rhetoric to becoming a suicide bomber, which creates a challenge to law enforcement. "Individuals can be radicalized in a number of ways—by direct contact with terrorists abroad or in the United States, over the Internet or on their own through a process of self-radicalization," said Assistant Attorney General David Kris, the top counterterrorism official at the Justice Department. These cases, Kris said, "underscore the constantly evolving nature of the threat we face."[4] Moreover, no single reason exists that attracts people to terrorism. According to Michael Chertoff, former Secretary of the Department of Homeland Security (DHS), "it's a combination of psychology, sociology, and people who, just for cultural reasons, gravitate" to Islamic extremism. We can't assume we've got months and years"[to apprehend them].[5]

---

[3] Ibid.
[4] Ibid.
[5] Ibid.

Radicalization Model—Evolving Causes

Islamic radicalization in the United States is an evolving model that requires close attention and careful review. Prior radicalization models concentrated on personal interactions between those who preach and propagate forceful action in the name of religion and those who are receptive to such a message. This personal interaction between the "enabler" and "potential recruit" still remains, with a caveat—modern communication technology has extended the reach of the enabler. According to numerous official statistics, there are disaffected, alienated people throughout the United States who, for decades, have joined gangs and cults in search of an identity. According to experts, radical Islamist groups are yet another destination for those who seek purpose in their lives.[6] In many cases, such individuals have no criminal record and can blend into society. These are the people who could be affected by a call to action by an "enabler," as they try to seek purpose in their lives.[7]

What some recent perpetrators of terrorist acts have in common is presence of community where the frustrated individual' views may have been discussed, enforced, strengthened, sharpened and ultimately, radicalized. Such is not the case of everyone. Fazal Shazad, the Times Square bomber, was not part of a notable Muslim community in Connecticut where he spent the last year before attempting to detonate an automobile laden with explosives. Therefore, a continuous update of radicalization metrics is necessary in discussing how one gets involved with the radical Islamic ideology. CTNSP's May 2008 study on the homegrown terrorism[8] identified a cluster of conditions that must be present for an individual to become radicalized. The effect is cumulative and iterative: removing one or more of these conditions may lower the radicalization level below the threshold required for violence. For example, an individual who is seeking an ideology, but who has no contact with a group and no particular grievance (i.e., has not been exposed to precipitants), will be unlikely to embrace terrorism (see figure 1.)

The CTNSP study on homegrown terrorism identified specific initiatives to counter and disrupt indoctrination tactics and methodologies, which were listed in the West Point Combating Terrorism Center.[9] In particular, the study encouraged law enforcement and intelligence community to exploit mistakes by radical Islamic jihadists. It also encouraged publicizing ideological retractors (leveraging the recanting of violence by former terrorists), as well as engaging mainstream Muslim clerics to issue fatwas (religious rulings) that incriminate the Jihadist Movement and their actions.

---

[6] http://www.homelandsecuritynewswire.com/noticeable-increase-number-americans-arrested-al-qaeda-related-terrorism?page=0,1

[7] Ibid. The cases of the "Lackawanna Six" and Coleen LaRose, discussed below, exemplify this trend

[8] Kimberley L. Thachuk, Marion E. "Spike" Bowman, and Courtney Richardson, *Homegrown Terrorism: the Threat Within*, Defense & Technology Paper 48 (Washington, D: Center For Technology and National Security Policy, May 2008).

[9] Jarret Brachman, Director of Research, West Point Combating Terrorism Center: "Abu Yahya's Six Easy Steps for Defeating Al-Qaeda."

Figure 1. Disrupting radicalization patterns.

What is changing in comparison with earlier cases and attempts is the time it takes individuals to become affiliated with more radical directions of Islamic ideology and to begin undertaking steps, which they believe is an inevitable goal of their new direction in life. Law enforcement and government agencies tasked with understanding, monitoring, and interdicting potential terrorist action must understand that the overall radicalization process is changing completely.

Pre-2009 general radicalization model involved individuals dedicated to their cause who lived, trained and received indoctrination, advice and support from within the Muslim community's radicalized elements.

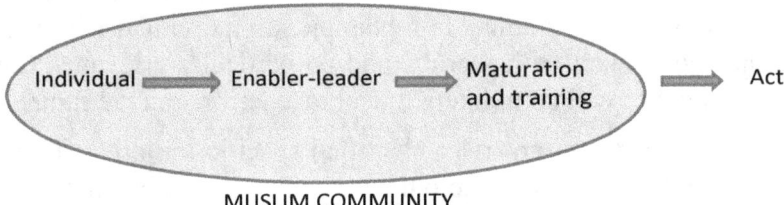

Present and future radicalization model takes the Muslim community and access to religious message into consideration, but does not require it – knowledge and radical Islamic message can be obtained from the Internet by an individual who was assimilated into larger American society.

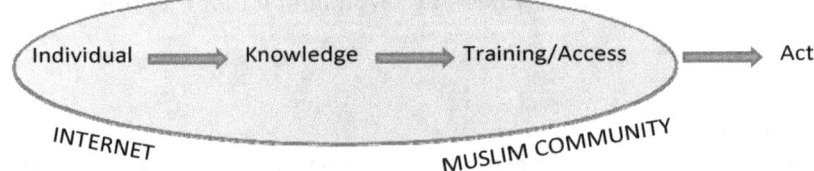

Figure 2. The changing nature of Islamic radicalization in the United States.

Analysis, resources, and technologies, were directed at recognizing, monitoring, and possibly identifying radicalized elements within the larger domestic Muslim community. It was believed that within large demographic concentrations of American Muslims, few disaffected, angered, or radicalized individuals could nurture their internal religious

8

struggle until it could be manifested in specific acts. At the same time, the largely peaceful and largely integrated American Muslim community provided an effective "screen" to these individuals by virtue of the perception that an entire ethnic/religious community in the United States does not intend to attack the American way of life by forceful and/or illegal means. In this context, gathering information on individuals within a larger community is not without problems and controversies, as concerns about security and intelligence gathering meet with the constitutional issues of human rights and discrimination.

Recent events have brought to light the evolving nature of an individual's relationship and interaction with radical versions of Islam. The larger community—the house of worship, family and friends, constant presence of cultural and social backgrounds—are no longer necessary. While in some cases, the community acts as a backdrop to an individual's perception of his or her role as a devout Muslim, in others it is the quest of the individual, far away from such community and connecting via Internet, that could lead to acts of terrorism. In such cases, individuals gain access to knowledge databases—radical teachings, sermons, preaching, essays, audio and video clips—available on various websites and content-sharing sites like YouTube. A leader who personally directs an individual toward more radicalized Islamic teachings may not be necessary at this crucial stage, making it harder for law enforcement to determine the origin and scope of motives that could lead to terrorist acts. Already in 2007, the intelligence community warned in an assessment that the spread of radical Internet websites and a growing number of self-generating cells in Western countries "indicate that the radical and violent segment of the West's Muslim population is expanding, including in the United States."[10] By mid-2010, recruitment efforts are not fully known, nor can they be accurately determined. According to Richard Nelson, a retired naval officer who served with the National Counterterrorism Center, points to the difficulty of tracking a trend that involves multiple groups with varying objectives.[11] What is now becoming clear is that past benchmarks for engaging, identifying, surveying, and interdicting potential domestic terrorists must be constantly updated to correspond with the evolving threat.

---

[10] http://www.google.com/hostednews/afp/article/ALeqM5izUS-A5r110g6r4KACilhLZE4myg
[11] Ibid.

Case Studies of Islamic Radicalization—Basic Trends and Principles

A. 9/11 Timeline and Implications for Future Understanding

It took the perpetrators of the 9/11 attacks from 4 to 7 years, depending on the individual, to travel the path from studying Islam to becoming radicalized by extremist ideology to indoctrination, planning, and execution of the terrorist act.[12] One of the key actors, Mohammed Atta, was introduced to observant Islam in 1994, when, while living in Germany, he went on a student trip to Turkey and Syria to research what would become his academic thesis on the conflict between Islam and modernity.[13] That same year, he made a pilgrimage to Mecca.[14] In 1995, he grew an Islamic-style beard, stopped listening to pop music and listened only to recitation of the Koran on tape. The following year, he began attending Al-Quds mosque in Hamburg.[15] The evidence shows that Atta and others were guided to their action by long-term, personal interaction and connection to Islamist individuals at mosques, safe houses, or training centers.

For all the men who planned attacks on American soil, years passed before they acted, during which time extensive religious debate, education, indoctrination, and planning took place. The culprits were interacting, congregating, and meeting at various American and international locales in order to plan their attack. They sought to avoid drawing much attention to their cause; their flight training ultimately did not arouse enough suspicion, as they sought to blend into the larger American society. The suspects often took part in joint activities, such as exercising at Florida gyms in the summer of 2001.[16] Most importantly, they did not vocalize or discuss their disappointment and anger with the Western world, and the United States in particular, with anyone outside their immediate contact circle. To carry out most of their activities, the men would often pay in cash, such as for vehicle or residence rental, to reduce the ability of authorities to track them.[17]

What is notable about their activities beginning approximately 1998—when some perpetrators and their associates started living and congregating together in Germany prior to moving to the United States—is their personal and direct connection to their cause, and the relatively basic use of modern communication technology like the Internet. They did not advertise or spread news of their planning via the worldwide web, nor did they post recruitment videos/websites to attract more followers to their cause. While it must be assumed that they knew their act would attract intense global attention, they nonetheless remained a close-knit group, preferring to maintain only low-level and minimal daily contact with everyone not associated with their cause. Once it became clear, through the process of indoctrination and personal interaction with their Islamist

---

[12] http://www.freerepublic.com/focus/news/683026/posts
[13] Ibid.
[14] Ibid.
[15] Ibid.
[16] Ibid.
[17] Ibid.

leaders and supporters, what role a particular individual would have in the impending attack the men carefully limited their interaction with most of the world around them.

This process underscores careful planning, premeditation, and extensive training over several years. Most of the conspirators were devout individuals who believed deeply in their cause. They were also separated from their families and all non-Muslim friends. The attackers occasionally "floated" onto law enforcement radars, but none of the men was ultimately flagged for accurate surveillance and apprehension. Had more robust interagency cooperation existed, perhaps various government agencies could have begun to piece together the picture of a terrorist conspiracy.

B.   2010 Attempted Times Square Bombing

The case of Fazal Shahzad, who attempted to detonate an explosive-laden SUV in the middle of New York City's Times Square, demonstrates the emergence of a different pattern, that of a fully integrated individual who, on the surface, and in the eyes of the larger community that surrounded him, drew no attention to himself. Unlike the 9/11 hijackers, many of whom assumed the trappings of the more conservative version of Islam, Shahzad did nothing of the sort. His operation outside the larger Muslim community presents tremendous difficulties for law enforcement to monitor and apprehend similar individuals; no fellow community member could have observed and possibly alerted the authorities in time. There was practically no suspicion for simple lack of evidence. This is the emerging scenario illustrated by figure 2.

Another disturbing fact is that Shahzad was at some point allegedly able to train with terrorists in Pakistan, return to the United States to assemble a car bomb in Connecticut, and park it in Times Square without anyone in the nation's counterterrorism apparatus knowing anything about it.[18] Since he did not belong to any known radical Islamic group, did not associate with or contact radical Islamic clerics, and did not spend time on known and monitored radical Islamic websites and chat rooms, he presents an example of an individual accessing the knowledge that leads him to ultimately commit the final act without requiring an enabler or mentor.

Following Shahzad's attempted attack, U.S. lawmakers suggested that there is a problem in the intelligence system that is difficult to fix. "Increasingly, the dilemma is the well-educated man who moves through the education system of our country somewhat promisingly," said Sen. Richard G. Lugar (R-Ind.). "I've always felt that this was the future in America for what we have to watch for in terrorism," said Sen. John D. Rockefeller IV (D-W.Va.), a member of the Senate Intelligence Committee. "And it's very hard to protect against, because you don't know who they are."[19] Additionally, the officials agreed that it was unlikely that questions would have been raised over Shahzad's apparently taking several trips to Pakistan, where his parents and other family members lived.

Shahzad is a graduate of U.S. universities and became a naturalized U.S. citizen in April 2009. He lived with his family in a quiet Connecticut suburb, and until last year was an

---

[18] http://www.washingtonpost.com/wp-dyn/content/article/2010/05/04/AR2010050405357 html
[19] Ibid.

employed homeowner. He broke no laws and did nothing to call attention to himself. So good was he at simply blending in with the rest of the American society that it was not until the day after the car bomb was found that Federal officials discovered a foreign connection, linking a telephone number used by the purchaser of the vehicle to Pakistan and, by early Monday morning, to Shahzad.[20] They gleaned details about him from an unrelated airport screening conducted when he returned from Pakistan in February, a requirement for all passengers from certain countries instituted after December 2009. The requirement was eliminated this spring after the targeted countries, including Pakistan, complained.[21]

Shahzad's radicalization timeline was much shorter than for the 9/11 suspects, which could have been no more than a year. According to the experts who inspected his car found in Times Square, Shahzad's training was "pitiful:" "There is less belief that he had any formal training or was a hardened militant," the Pakistani official interviewed by New York daily News said. "He might have gotten some briefings, but not much."[22] "Hardcore" militants typically get about 5 to 6 months of training at modest camps near Afghanistan, officials said. Shahzad's shorter time in North Waziristan's most notorious towns wasn't enough for advanced terror instruction, the officials added.[23] "It doesn't seem like he was there long enough," a second U.S. counterterrorism official confirmed.[24]

Whether Shahzad did not apply all he may have learnt in Pakistan, or whether he was not taught enough to properly construct a car bomb, the fact remains that in a relatively short time, this young man was able to place a deadly device that could have had as great an effect on New York City as the 9/11 attack, which was elaborately planned for many years. There may be repeats of such an act, as disaffected and radicalized Muslims in the United States opt to finish Shahzad's mission. In such a scenario, the interdiction mission for domestic law enforcement would be exponentially complicated.

C.   Lackawanna Six—the Case of Yemeni-Americans from Upstate New York.

In the case of the six young Muslim-American men who traveled to Afghanistan from Lackawanna, New York, to receive terrorist training, the presence of a charismatic leader-enabler was crucial in pushing these young men in the direction of radicalized Islam. They were U.S. citizens bound together by their Yemeni heritage, went to Lackawanna High School and played soccer for the varsity team, and largely kept to themselves.[25] They traveled to Yemen once a year, to the village of their heritage.[26] Up

---

[20] Ibid.
[21] Ibid.
[22] http://www nydailynews.com/news/ny_crime/2010/05/30/2010-05-
30_why_faisal_bombed_trained_in_taliban_cities_but_didnt_get_full_course_sez_pro html
[23] Ibid.
[24] Ibid.
[25] http://www.washingtonpost.com/wp-dyn/content/article/2007/09/07/AR2007090702049_pf.html
[26] Ibid.

until that point, the young boys were able to assimilate and integrate into American society. Following high school graduation, their lives took a turn toward petty crime, low-level jobs, and drift. This lack of direction made them perfect targets for radical Islamist recruiting.[27]

Their main recruiter was an al-Qaeda operative named Kamal Derwish. An American who had moved from Lackawanna to Saudi Arabia as a child, Derwish called the small steel town's Muslim community "virgin territory."[28] He told the men that if they ever expected to be good Muslims, they would have to sign onto jihad.[29] Significant signs of the boys' radicalization included private meetings hosted by Derwish, who acted as the spiritual sanctioner and sought to create a bond between the boys in a place where they could freely discuss and study his version of religion. This was achieved by such activities as pizza and wrestling matches and was augmented by withdrawal from their mosque.[30] Once the young men were relatively isolated from their familiar environment, they embarked on the road that would lead them to Afghanistan.

After their indoctrination, seven U.S. citizens—Yaseinn Taher, Yahya Goba, Shafel Mosed, Mukhtar al-Bakri, Sahim Alwan, Faysal Galab, and Jaber Elbaneh—left for jihad training in Afghanistan in April-August 2001.[31] They told friends they were going to Pakistan for religious instruction. Escorted by Derwish, the men traveled separately and attended a 6-week weapons course at the Al Farooq camp.[32]

Just two days after some of them have arrived, two of the seven, Sahim Alwan and Jaber Elbaneh, and Derwish met briefly with Osama bin Laden in a small group setting. One of the men asked bin Laden about a rumor that something big is about to happen. Bin Laden responded: "They're threatening us. And we're threatening them. But there are brothers willing to carry their souls in their hands."[33] A couple of weeks later, the seven Lackawanna men and Derwish began their training camp near Kandahar.[34] One day, bin Laden and Ayman al-Zawahiri came to their camp and bin Laden gave a speech in Arabic to the hundreds of trainees. In his 20-minute speech, he discussed the merger between al-Qaeda and Islamic Jihad.[35] At the end, he called on the gathering to pray for the 40 operatives who were en route for a very important mission.[36]

In early June 2001, the Buffalo, New York, FBI field office received an anonymous, handwritten letter from someone in the Yemeni community of Lackawanna, near Buffalo. The letter said that a group has traveled to "meet bin Laden and stay in his camp for

---

[27] Ibid.

[28] Ibid.

[29] Ibid.

[30] http://www manhattan-institute.org/html/cpt.htm

[31] http://www historycommons.org/timeline.jsp?complete_911_timeline_al_qaeda_by_region=complete_91 1_timeline__lackawanna_six_&timeline=complete_911_timeline

[32] Ibid.

[33] Ibid.

[34] Ibid.

[35] Ibid.

[36] Bid.

training."[37] The person who wrote it added, "I can not give you my name because I fear for my life." It said that "two terrorists" have been recruiting in Lackawanna, and that eight men have gone to train in Afghanistan, and four more were planning to go later.[38] The letter gave the names of the men, who at that time were already in an al-Qaeda training camp in Afghanistan. The letter was assigned to FBI agent Edward Needham, the only Buffalo agent at this time working on counterterrorism. He ran the names through criminal databases and found that many of them had criminal records for drug dealing and cigarette smuggling.[39] He was skeptical that drug dealers would fight for al-Qaeda, but he sent the letter up the chain of command and opened an investigation on June 15, 2001.[40] Three of the suspects—Faysal Galab, Shafel Mosed, and Yaseinn Taher—were stopped on June 27, 2001 when they arrived in New York on a flight back from Pakistan, because Needham put their names on an FBI watch list.[41] They were questioned for 2 hours and released.

Around July 2001, Needham interviewed Sahim Alwan, who had recently come back from Afghanistan. But Alwan said he had only traveled to Pakistan for religious training.[42] The others who returned also failed to tell any authorities that they had been in Afghanistan or what they learned there.[43] On September 11, 2001, hours after the 9/11 attacks, Needham called Alwan and asked him if anyone new had come into town. Alwan answered in the negative.[44] But in fact, Juma al-Dosari, an al-Qaeda operative who recruited the Lackawanna Six, had recently returned to Lackawanna, and Alwan knew where he was staying.[45] Al-Dosari was trying to recruit a second group of young men to train in Afghanistan. The training camps were closed down, and al-Dosari left town before the FBI found out he was there.[46]

In November 2001, al-Dosari was captured in Afghanistan and later transferred to the Guantanamo prison. During interrogation, in the spring of 2002, he revealed several aliases and that he was trying to recruit a group of U.S. citizens in New York State known as the "Lackawanna Six."[47] In September 2002, the Lackawanna group was arrested by U.S. authorities.

The Lackawanna Six spent several months in indoctrination and several months in actual training—again, their timeline is significantly shorter than for the 9/11 attackers, though certain parallels exist. They did not seek out radical Islamic doctrine on their own. Rather, they were recruited by an al-Qaeda affiliated individual who correctly assumed that their status as petty criminal and drifters without a cause made them ripe for "re-

---

[37] Ibid.
[38] Ibid.
[39] Ibid.
[40] Ibid.
[41] Ibid.
[42] Ibid.
[43] Ibid.
[44] Ibid.
[45] Ibid.
[46] Ibid.
[47] Ibid.

packaging." Without such an enabler, these young men might have continued their lives as petty criminals. Their recruiter ensured that his students were surrounded by a radicalized "community," his own apartment away from the rest of the people or at terrorist training camps in remote Afghanistan. Even after an anonymous tip from the Lackawanna community, the FBI remained skeptical of a terrorist connection, given that the men in question possessed no radical background. Had a better relationship existed between local and state law enforcement representatives and the Lackawanna Muslim community, perhaps the al-Qaeda recruiters would not have been able to operate in what was considered an open playing field for potential radicalization.

D. Self-indoctrination—the Case of "Jihad Jane," or Coleen Rene LaRose[48]

Coleen Larose was arrested October 16, 2009, after landing at the Philadelphia International Airport on a flight from the Netherlands. Federal authorities stated that LaRose, who had previously converted to Islam and become a militant Jihadist, flew to Europe on August 23, 2009, with the intent to live and train with Muslim jihadists in a plot to find and kill Swedish artist Lars Vilks, whose 2007 portrait of the prophet Muhammad as a dog angered many Muslims.[49]

In 1980 at the age of 16, Colleen LaRose married a man in Fort Worth, Texas, who was twice her age. Reportedly, her husband was physically and mentally abusive, and the marriage did not last long. Police records indicate that Colleen LaRose had a history of misdemeanor violations, beginning with a charge of criminal trespass in 1985. She was charged with drunken driving in 1997; that same year she was arrested for passing four bad checks that totaled to $390.71.[50] Her petty crime and unstable financial and personal situation, as with the Lackawanna Six, made her an attractive recruit into the radicalized part of Islam.

In 1988, she married Rodolfo Cavazos, a gambler. That marriage ended in divorce after 10 years. Caught in a life of mounting bills, little money, an unstable second marriage, and an addiction to alcohol, she became a person living on the "edge of personal destruction."[51] On May 21, 2005, depressed over her father's recent death, LaRose began drinking heavily. In a failed suicide attempt, she swallowed 8–10 pills of a prescription muscle relaxant.[52] After months of counseling for depression and alcoholism, LaRose apparently found spiritual rebirth in Islam.[53]

---

[48] LaRose is not to be confused with another "Jihad Jane," Nada Nadim Prouty, a naturalized American citizen who was arrested by U.S. authorities for ties to Hezbollah and for compromising FBI and CIA intelligence operations.

[49] http://www.examiner.com/x-21743-St-John-the-Baptist-Parish-Progressive-Examiner~y2010m3d13-When-looks-can-kill-The-Story-of-Jihad-Jane-AKA-Colleen-Renee-LaRose

[50] Ibid.

[51] Ibid.

[52] Ibid.

[53] Ibid.

Unlike previous terrorist suspects and perpetrators, and possibly like many future attackers, Colleen LaRose freely visited Internet-based radical Islamic websites, using the alias "Jihad Jane."[54] On the Internet, she openly and angrily called for Muslims worldwide to rise in "Holy War" against the United States and the West; her web-based activities caught the attention of U.S. law enforcement as a person of interest to watch.[55] LaRose allegedly wrote in an email message that it would be "an honor and great pleasure to die or kill for" Islamic holy war.[56] Federal authorities claim LaRose raised funds for militant groups, arranged for false travel documents, and used Internet postings to recruit people to carry out violent attacks.[57] U.S. Attorney Michael L. Levy, at a news conference about LaRose, said the woman was "another very real danger lurking on the Internet" and that the blonde, blue-eyed woman's alleged acts "shatter any lingering thought that we can spot a terrorist based on appearance."[58]

To friends and neighbors, LaRose's transformation came as a shock, much like for those who knew Fazal Shahzad for most of his American life. According to those that know her, she was a polite yet eccentric woman who was known to talk loudly to her cats and on occasion indulged in hard drinking.[59] It is also important to point out that like Shahzad, she did not otherwise draw attention to herself by exhibiting any type of conservative Islamic dress or code of conduct.

---

[54] Ibid.
[55] Ibid.
[56] http://www.upi.com/Daily-Briefing/2010/03/10/Jihad-Jane/UPI-41871268228371/
[57] Ibid.
[58] Ibid.
[59] http://www.examiner.com/x-21743-St-John-the-Baptist-Parish-Progressive-Examiner~y2010m3d13-When-looks-can-kill-The-Story-of-Jihad-Jane-AKA-Colleen-Renee-LaRose.

The Power of Technology in Radicalization

There appears to be emerging a dispersed model of radicalization and recruitment. Rather than follow a more defined and interpersonal path from interest in religion to committing acts of violence in its name, there is now a "self-regulating" model. While some acts of terror are committed following personal, face-to-face indoctrination by religious leaders and figureheads that are conducted in specific physical locations around the world, it is now becoming possible to absorb religious material and "call to arms" through readily accessible, electronic media, such as video sharing and social networking sites—YouTube alone has numerous videos designed to educate, indoctrinate, and persuade those wishing to explore their options or test their faith. Such new ways of disseminating propaganda are causing great concern to law enforcement agencies, both domestic and international, as it targets not just a small, devout religious following, but potentially millions of users.

The threat potential for Internet-dissemination of a radical Islamic agenda has been recognized by U.S. government organizations tasked with homeland security. The U.S. Senate Committee on Homeland Security and Government Affairs issued a report in 2008 on violent Islamist extremism and the Internet.[60] In the report, the committee recognized that the Internet plays an important role during the radicalization process—as individuals progress through the various stages of radicalization, their use of the Internet evolves as well. This initiative made use of the New York City Police Department's own report, "Radicalization in the West: The Homegrown Threat," which identified four radicalization stages. In the second, or self-identification, phase, the Internet serves chiefly as the person's source of information about Islam and a venue to meet other seekers online.[61] With the current aggressive proliferation of the jihadi-Salafi ideology online, it is nearly impossible for someone to avoid this extreme interpretation of Islam when inquiring about Islam as a religion.

During the indoctrination phase, those undergoing self-administered brainwashing devote their time in the cyber world to extremist sites and chat rooms—tapping into virtual networks of like-minded individuals around the world who reinforce the individual's beliefs and commitment and further legitimize them.[62] Coleen LaRose participated in this process for years. At this stage, individuals or the groups they are in are likely to begin proliferating jihadi-Salafist ideology online along with consuming it. The Internet becomes a virtual "echo chamber"—acting as a radicalization accelerant while creating the path for the ultimate stage of jihadization.[63] In the jihadization phase, people challenge and encourage each others' move to action, with the Internet now a tactical

---

[60] May 8, 2008 Report by the Majority and Minority staff of the Senate Committee on Homeland Security and Governmental Affairs Committee on the threat of homegrown terrorism inspired by violent Islamist extremism. http://hsgac.senate.gov/public/_files/IslamistReport.pdf
[61] Ibid.
[62] Ibid.
[63] Ibid.

resource for obtaining instructions on constructing weapons, gathering information on potential targets, and providing spiritual justification for an attack.[64]

A good example of this Internet-based phenomenon, where domestic reach can quickly grow into an international message, is the case of the Russian citizen Alexander Tikhomirov (who went by the Islamic name Sayid Buryatski), who inspired two female suicide bombers to target the Moscow subway in March 2010. There are more than a dozen YouTube videos of him offering educational and ecumenical information in the Russian language.[65] Anyone who wants to hear this man's message and his take on Islam and non-believers can do so at the click of a button. There are numerous videos of Tikhomirov's speeches, with comments of support or disdain offered by what looks like an international audience. Additionally, any YouTube search on Islam as a religion not only yields a massive database of knowledge, but turns up advocacy of Islam's superiority to other religions by showing examples of conversions by Christians, Jews, and people from other religions. Utilizing the way that YouTube matches similar or linked videos together on the screen for ease of use by the inquirer, clicking successively on these videos can ultimately lead to information that offers a more stern and inflexible interpretation of Islam. Many YouTube channels also feature numerous clips that offer a wide religious spectrum, from entertainment to education to serious dialogue to claims of Islam's superiority over other religions.

This raises an uncomfortable point—how can potentially extremist propaganda be checked and properly monitored in a completely free information environment when even videos that incite religious discord are openly and repeatedly posted online? Should not the fight against technologically advanced extremism be concentrated at its informational source, such as the Internet, and YouTube in particular? What rules and regulations exist with YouTube, for example, as the dominant network of this kind that would allow for control and interdiction of extremist propaganda? As long as anyone can freely locate videos that feature calls to religious martyrdom, jihad, and war against non-Muslims, the majority of state and international efforts are doomed to lag behind those of radicalized individuals who wish to take the fight into their own hands.

Other kinds of modern technology aid and abet the spread of web-based extremist propaganda, from smart phones to personal computing devices. The ease with which web-based content can be accessed at virtually any time and anywhere in the world impedes both domestic and international law enforcement efforts to undercut the spread of such unwelcome information. Therefore, it becomes essential to cut off access to such information at its source—but the freedom of information law and principles that apply to the Internet/YouTube content restrict such action. On occasion, we hear of more extreme videos taken down due to complaints, but for every video of the kind taken down, others remain, like the two below of Adam Ghadahn, "American Taliban."

---

[64] Ibid.

[65] http://www.youtube.com/watch?v=dLMWueOuExQ (Tikhomirov seems to be sitting in front of a barrel that has been refashioned into a bomb, stating that "this is a "present" to the Nazran (Russian) security forces.")

Adam Gadahn (Azzam Al-Amriki) on the Pakistani Government 2/4
http://www.youtube.com/watch?v=Q8S_0RFq4Nw&feature=related

Al-Qaida Calls on U.S. Muslims to Attack America
http://www.youtube.com/watch?v=BBmhKutfJ48

The apprehension of "Jihad Jane"—a white, middle-aged convert to Islam—illustrates the point that access to and dissemination of radical Islamist propaganda can incite unlikely people to acts of terror against non-Muslims. International law enforcement efforts can limit the spread or presence of perpetrators of terrorism by physically taking custody of individuals who advocate violence and conflict—but as long as their messages can be freely seen and read on the Internet, more and more people will be drawn to combat in the name of Islam.

A recent example illustrates the power and reach of Internet-based radical Islamist propaganda. An online blogger who targeted the creators of the American *South Park* animated series for satirizing issues surrounding the depiction of the Prophet Muhammad has distributed jihadist materials and promoted violence against non-Muslims through a variety of online platforms for at least a year.[66] Abu Talhah Al-Amrikee, the username of the blogger who identified himself as Zachary A. Chesser in January 2010, publicized terrorist propaganda, endorsed suicide attacks, and espoused hatred against Jews, Israel, and Shi'a Muslims through a variety of websites, blogs, and social networking sites. "The jihad movement has moved from the mountains and caves to the bedrooms of every major city around the world," Chesser wrote in a March 2010 post to the website of Revolution Muslim (RM), a fringe, anti-Semitic Muslim organization that justifies terrorist attacks and other forms of violence against non-Muslims.[67]

On April 15, 2010, the morning after the offensive episode of South Park aired, Chesser made his first comment about the program on his Twitter feed. "May Allah kill Matt Stone and Trey Parker (show creators and chief animators) and burn them in Hell for all eternity. They insult our prophets Muhammad, Jesus, and Moses ...."[68] Chesser posted a similar entry to his Mujahid Blog on the same day. The post included a picture of the assassination of Dutch filmmaker Theo Van Gogh by a Muslim extremist in 2004 with the caption: "Theo Van Gogh—Have Matt Stone And Trey Parker Forgotten This?"[69] In the post, Chesser provided the address to Stone and Parker's offices, telling readers to "contact them" or "pay Comedy Central ... a visit."[70] Chesser also noted: "We have to warn Matt and Trey that what they are doing is stupid and they will probably wind up like Theo Van Gogh if they do air this show. This is not a threat, but a warning of the reality of what will likely happen to them."[71] As of the time of writing, June 2010, the

---

[66] http://www.adl.org/main_Terrorism/abu_talhah htm
[67] Ibid.
[68] Ibid.
[69] Ibid.
[70] Ibid.
[71] Ibid.

www.RevolutionMuslim.com website is still up and operational, delivering its opinion to anyone who logs on.

The Internet was the chosen radicalization tool of Coleen LaRose, who used primarily YouTube and MySpace, the latter featuring pictures of her in both a hijab and burqa, items her neighbors in Pennsylvania never saw her wear.[72] At the time of writing, police and intelligence services in 10 countries in North America, Europe, Asia and Africa were investigating a plot apparently conceived, planned, and brought down on the Internet.[73] Sometime in June 2008, a "couple of months" after she had "reverted" to Islam, LaRose made her first, significant Internet move when she posted a video on YouTube using the pseudonym "Jihad Jane," saying she was "desperate to do something somehow to help" ease the suffering of Muslims.[74] People then began to email her via YouTube and, later, her MySpace page, where she listed "Sheikh OBL [Osama bin Laden] and the brothers in jihad" among her heroes.[75]

In December 2008, LaRose is alleged to have received an email from an unnamed male admirer in South Asia saying he wanted to become a "shaheed" or martyr. She replied the following day that she, too, wanted to die in holy war.[76] Over the course of the following months, Ms LaRose is said to have been in Internet contact with at least five would-be terrorists in Asia, North America, and Europe, including at least one in Ireland.[77] By March 2009, another correspondent in South Asia had proposed killing Lars Vilks, the Swedish cartoonist who enraged Muslims worldwide in 2007 with one of his drawings.[78] He emailed Ms LaRose that Mr. Vilks should be killed "in a way that the whole kufar world would get frightened." She replied: "I will make this my goal or die trying."[79]

He also told Ms LaRose that, as a blonde, blue-eyed American, she "could get access to many places." He suggested that she "marry me to get me inside Europe."[80] According to the U.S. indictment, she agreed and began making plans to go to Sweden. It is believed that much correspondence was conducted through a single email account—a so-called "blind drop," where multiple users share one password, leaving messages in the drafts folder, so that key information never gets transmitted or caught up in web filters.[81] In August 2009, Ms LaRose removed the hard drive from her computer, stole her boyfriend's passport, and flew to Europe.[82] She was arrested when she returned to the United States in mid-October 2009.[83] Her online activities, however, had long been the

[72] http://www.thenational.ae/apps/pbcs.dll/article?AID=/20100317/FOREIGN/703169948/1013/ART
[73] Ibid.
[74] Ibid.
[75] Ibid.
[76] Ibid.
[77] Ibid.
[78] Ibid.
[79] Ibid.
[80] Ibid.
[81] Ibid.
[82] Ibid.
[83] Ibid.

subject of interest to a band of amateur Internet investigators who dedicate their online time to tracking down potential terrorists, child abusers, and other criminals.

Members of two such groups, the Jawa Report and the YouTube Smackdown Corps, claim to have been tracking Ms LaRose's online postings as early as 2007.[84] Originally, they regarded her online, anti-American, anti-Zionist rants as something of a joke, but in 2009, when she is said to have appealed for funds to support terrorist activity through her postings on Twitter, one Jawa contributor reported her to the FBI.[85] Agents interviewed her shortly before her abrupt departure for Europe, but she denied any knowledge of "Jihad Jane." She avoided arrest on that occasion, but fortunately was on the U.S. security services' radar.

The American man who reported Ms LaRose to the authorities in July 2009 (he does not want to be identified), said he had been tracking her for about a year and a half.[86] He first encountered her after watching a YouTube channel dedicated to Middle Eastern performing arts: "One thing led to another and the next thing I knew, I was dealing with fanatics such as Jihad Jane/Fatima LaRose, whose real identity was later revealed as Colleen LaRose."[87]

He said Ms LaRose "recklessly" posted information about herself on websites. "Her previous internet activity was easy to track.[88] In it she listed her real name, birth date, location, and even online pictures of herself," he added. "Although YouTube Smackdown was responsible for removing most of her terrorist accounts, she remained determined to create more accounts on YouTube promoting terrorism against the United States.[89] "She got more of a following of real terrorists as time went on, joining online terrorist websites and promoting them on her YouTube channels," said the source. "When she finally made an account which actively solicited funds for the Pakistan Mujaheddin, which I knew she had acquired the contacts for, I knew she had become a real threat to our safety."[90]

The above-mentioned examples represent a small portion of the way the Internet augments the dissemination and access to violent, radicalized, Islamist propaganda that calls for acts of physical harm to Americans and Westerners. These examples are also a tip of the iceberg, since they feature English-language content. It is known that numerous websites and Internet-based content exist in other languages all over the world. What is significant is that, previously, very few Americans could freely access and understand this content—especially if it was in another language. Today, more and more English-language data is targeting potential American audiences. Dealing with such an information stream requires both resiliency and resolve on the part of U.S. local, state, and Federal authorities.

---

[84] Ibid.
[85] Ibid.
[86] Ibid.
[87] Ibid.
[88] Ibid.
[89] Ibid.
[90] Ibid.

Current efforts to police massive, content-sharing sites like YouTube fall short of removing videos and films that act as recruitment tools. When it comes to U.S. government efforts, there are only limited results. In May 2008, U.S. Senator Joseph Lieberman, chairman of the Senate Homeland Security and Governmental Affairs Committee, asked Google CEO Eric Schmidt in an open letter to remove Islamic terrorist videos from YouTube, which is owned by Google.[91] Islamic terrorist organizations, Lieberman said, use YouTube to distribute propaganda, attract followers, and provide weapons training.[92] While YouTube has community guidelines for its users, Lieberman said "it does not appear that [Google] is enforcing these guidelines to the extent they would apply to [terrorist] content.[93] According to the Senator's findings, "searches on YouTube return dozens of videos branded with an icon or logo identifying the videos as the work of one of these Islamist terrorist organizations," Lieberman said. "A great majority of these videos document horrific attacks on American soldiers in Iraq or Afghanistan. Others provide weapons training, speeches by al-Qaeda leadership, and general material intended to radicalize potential recruits."[94]

The results were split between YouTube's need for transparency in its global operations and security concerns by a senior U.S. legislator, which ultimately fell short of attempting to remove questionable content from the website. At the time, the company replied that "Senator Lieberman stated his belief, in a letter, that all videos mentioning or featuring these groups should be removed from YouTube—even legal nonviolent or non-hate speech videos. While we respect and understand his views, YouTube encourages free speech and defends everyone's right to express unpopular points of view. We believe that YouTube is a richer and more relevant platform for users precisely because it hosts a diverse range of views, and rather than stifle debate we allow our users to view all acceptable content and make up their own minds."[95]

Following Senator Lieberman's efforts and wide-ranging debate on the issue, YouTube changed its Community Guidelines by adding language prohibiting the posting of videos "inciting others to commit violent acts."[96] These Community Guidelines assist YouTube's internal monitoring team to review flagged videos for removal. The larger issue, however, is whether YouTube's internal monitoring effort is effective enough, since the company only reviews videos flagged by YouTube viewers that may violate the Community Guidelines. "The core underlying issue," said Ben Venzke of Intel Center, a private sector contractor that monitors extremist web communications for clients, including the U.S. government, "is that whether you take these videos off YouTube or not, they will always be available at numerous other locations online. New outlets are popping up constantly, and when you take one down, 10 more simply appear to fill the gap. The problem is the very nature of the Internet itself. It makes controlling and

---

[91] http://www.informationweek.com/news/internet/google/showArticle.jhtml?articleID=207801148
[92] Ibid.
[93] Ibid.
[94] Ibid.
[95] Ibid.
[96] http://www.youtube.com/t/community_guidelines

denying access to information simply impossible."[97] Many of the videos highlighted by Senator Lieberman's office that were produced by al-Qaida's media arms in Iraq and Afghanistan "show attacks on U.S. forces in which American soldiers are injured and, in some cases, killed," wrote Lieberman.[98] While many roadside bomb attacks against coalition vehicles were shown in the mid-distance, there were plenty of other videos that showed more graphic scenes. But John Morris, senior counsel at the Center for Democracy and Technology, noted that "top-selling movies also have scenes depicting extreme violence" and that it was appropriate that YouTube should enforce its own guidelines.[99] In what is perhaps the best evidence of the evolving nature and tactics of the domestic terrorist threat over the past several years, intelligence specialists at the time told the press that "Lieberman is barking up the wrong tree. Removing material from YouTube would have little to no effect on key terrorist groups' primary dissemination efforts. There are no major jihadi groups … using YouTube as their primary release point."[100] While these specialists may have been right at the time, several arrests suggest that the domestic threat may not be coming from "major jihadi groups," but from individuals with no direct connections to international terrorist networks.

At the time of writing, another group of individuals was apprehended by the authorities for planning to wage Jihad against the American people and U.S. interests. On June 6, 2010, two New Jersey men who envisioned a terrorist attack in the United States with a body count twice that of the Fort Hood massacre were arrested at New York's Kennedy Airport, as they were about to board flights on their way to Somalia to seek terror training from al-Qaida-affiliated jihadists.[101] Mohamed Mahmood Alessa, 20, and Carlos Eduardo Almonte, 26, were arrested before they could board separate flights to Egypt and then continue on to Somalia, according to Federal officials in New Jersey and the New York Police Department.[102] The two men tried to get recruited by Islamic radicals on their own, and had traveled to Jordan in 2007 to get into Iraq, but were turned back by their intended recruiters. Since then, during the lengthy investigation, an NYPD undercover officer recorded conversations with the men in which they spoke about jihad against Americans.[103] "I leave this time. God willing, I never come back," authorities say Alessa told the officer last year. "Only way I would come back here is if I was in the land of jihad and the leader ordered me to come back here and do something here. Ah, I love that."[104]

According to the Associated Press, they had no known connections to terrorist groups, and their planned trip to Somalia apparently amounted to a leap of faith that they would be embraced by the jihadists. Investigators say they are among many U.S. terrorism suspects to have been inspired by two well-known U.S. citizens who have recruited

[97] http://www.upi.com/Top_News/Special/2008/05/20/Analysis-Should-YouTube-censor-al-Qaida/UPI-60601211292733/
[98] Ibid.
[99] Ibid.
[100] Ibid.
[101] http://www.star-telegram.com/2010/06/06/2243660/two-terrorism-suspects-arrested.html
[102] Ibid.
[103] http://news.yahoo.com/s/ap/20100607/ap_on_re_us/us_terrorism_arrests
[104] Ibid.

terrorists through the Internet: Adam Gadahn, an al-Qaida spokesman in Pakistan, and Anwar al-Awlaki, a radical al-Qaida cleric hiding in Yemen, who is believed to have helped inspire recent attacks, including the Fort Hood shooting, the Times Square bombing attempt, and the failed Christmas Day 2009 airline bombing.[105] The FBI received a tip regarding the men's activities in October 2006, according to the U.S. Attorney's office in New Jersey. The tip, from someone who knew the men, said, "Every time they access the Internet all they look for is all those terrorist videos. ... They keep saying that Americans are their enemies, that everybody other than Islamic followers are their enemies ... and they all must be killed."[106] While the two men did not make sophisticated preparations for their intended activities, what is crucial here is that young, impressionable American citizens were influenced by the radicalized information found freely on the Internet to such a degree that they were willing to undertake a complicated journey to Somalia to join the ranks of Al-Shahab, a violent, Islamist extremist group, to target the American people.

---

[105] Ibid.
[106] http://www.cnn.com/2010/CRIME/06/06/new.york.terror.arrests/?hpt=T2

Conclusions

At this point, U.S. government agencies are well aware of the magnitude of risk that is posed by the evolving domestic radicalization fueled by an extreme version of Islam. Specifically, the Department of Homeland Security has an Extremism and Radicalization Branch within the Homeland Environment Threat Analysis Division (Office of Intelligence and Analysis). In studying radicalization, DHS is working closely with Federal, state, and local partners and is focusing on a wide range of actors and organizations both Islamic—those who try to gain legitimacy by illegitimately wrapping themselves within Islam—and non-religious extremists.[107] This initiative has yielded key finds, among which is the recognition that "Lone-wolf" radicalization is not unique to any particular ideology, and the ease of mass communications portends an increase in acts of terror by violent individuals. Formal affiliation with a group is not essential to radicalization, nor is it essential to being trained, obtaining resources, or otherwise supporting an operational capability.[108]

When it comes to people willing to join the ranks of violent extremist organizations influenced by radical Islamist teachings, we are witnessing an evolution of sorts in methods, tactics, and most importantly, "idea proliferation" in the United States. In some examples presented here, an older model of radicalization was discussed. For the 9/11 and Lackawanna Six perpetrators, the process of indoctrination, radicalization, training, and planning took place over years and was done with the direct participation of specific Islamic figures, who mentored, supported, encouraged, and led the men towards their final act. The perpetrators belonged to Muslim communities, and while their degree of religiosity differed substantially, they were nonetheless radicalized and encouraged in the atmosphere of extreme religious teaching, either in the United States or abroad. In the case of the Lackawanna Six, they were recruited by Al Qaeda representatives themselves, whose stated goal was to recruit American Muslims for acts of terrorism. On the other hand, Shahzad and LaRose present a different dilemma, with LaRose exemplifying a new trend, where the Internet can act as a powerful amplifier of radical Islamic teachings. If the overall radicalization trends discussed in the paper are mapped out, the following trend emerges, as illustrated by figure 3.

---

[107] 2007 written testimony by Charles Allen, Assistant Secretary for Intelligence and Analysis at the DHS, speaking to the Senate Committee on Homeland Security and Government Affairs on the "Threat of Islamic Radicalization to the Homeland."
http://www.investigativeproject.org/documents/testimony/270.pdf
[108] Ibid.

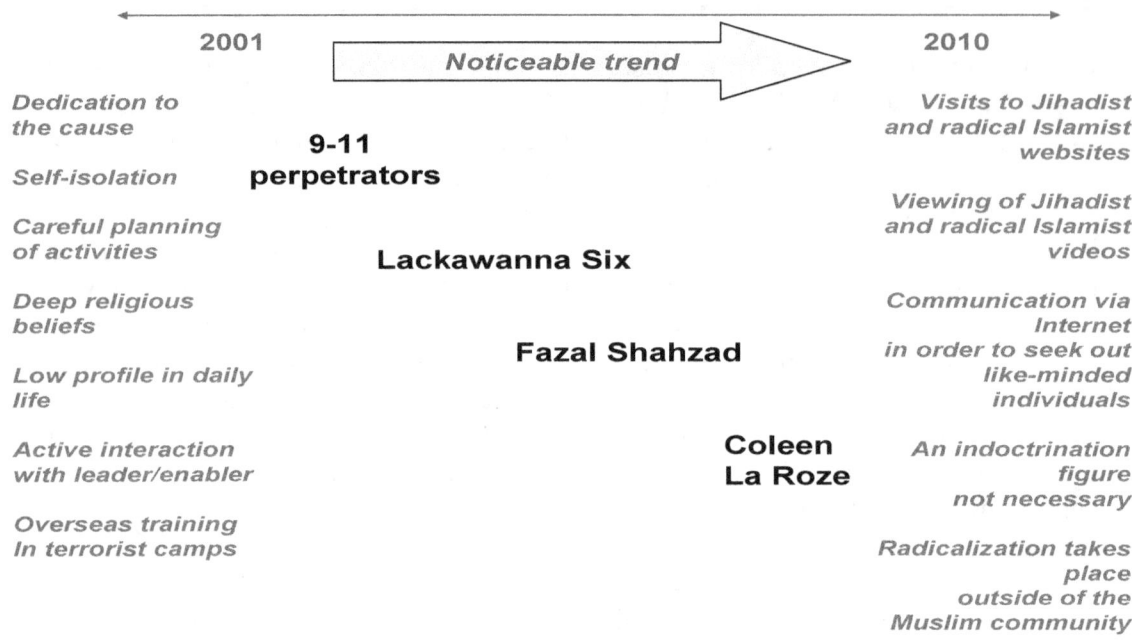

Figure 3. Changing nature of Islamic radicalization trends in the United States

Several key factors that were important for the 9/11 perpetrators are absent for the latest suspects. It can be expected—and indeed the law enforcement community is already concerned—that the next potential terrorists will come from the larger American society, and will not draw attention to themselves until it is too late to stop them. It must be noted that Shahzad's bomb could have worked, and it was only by chance that he was apprehended at the airport as he prepared to flee the country.

The common elements that can be mapped out for the four above-mentioned cases are that the suspects and perpetrators were:
- Dissatisfied with their lives;
- Indoctrinated, either overseas or in the United States;
- Trained, either overseas or locally;
- Separated from the larger Muslim community and their families, which had no part in their path towards radicalization.
- Radicalized largely via the Internet, especially in the most recent cases.

It is, therefore, essential to assess the emerging trends in domestic radicalization and treat this menace not just as a law enforcement issue, but as information warfare. The discussion, communication, and interaction over the Internet that targets the United States and its core values now take place in English, and very specific content is now aimed at American audiences with websites, videos, and messages. This is a major difference form the earlier communication and indoctrination tools, when the potential terrorists had to be present in Muslim countries and territories for training and preparation. Such activity

26

would draw domestic and international attention from entities responsible for interdicting such actions.

Today, that dynamic is changing—Coleen LaRose, Alessa, and Almonte exemplify the new trend, and Shahzad reinforces it by virtue of being considered a successful, assimilated naturalized U.S. citizen with perceived loyalties to the United States and its value system. If this new trend is reinforced by the Internet, then the American law enforcement and intelligence communities must target the source and dissemination tactics of radicalized Islamist propaganda—the websites, chat rooms, and Internet videos that spread such messages. Such information outlets must be shut down, taken out of commission, removed from servers, and otherwise disabled in order to minimize potential exposure to its hateful content by impressionable or desperate individuals. The proliferation of such Internet-based content can be greatly reinforced by a variety of new technologies like smart phones; as long as such information remains in the open, it can potential recruit numerous individuals to undertake radical actions.

Recommendations

The growing threat posed by domestic radicalization, coupled with the difficulty of identifying/spotting/interdicting individuals who embark on the path of violence against U.S. territory and citizens, is revitalizing the debate on domestic intelligence gathering. In order for the public to be protected against violent acts of terrorism, key and specific information has to be targeted by the nation's law enforcement bodies to properly analyze and interdict the emerging threat. In some cases, the threat may have matured to the point of individuals embarking on the final stages of preparation for an attack. Therefore, a wide ranging effort is necessary which takes into account people's backgrounds, communities, contacts, interests, and interactions in order to get a better "visual" on the potential or real threat.

There is a growing difficulty in gathering adequate intelligence on domestic acts of terrorism. As noted in the case of the recent attempt to bomb Times Square, there were few pieces of data that an intelligence analyst would have been able to assemble "to zero in on a suspect," according to Los Angeles Police Department counterterrorism chief Michael Downing.[109] Currently, DHS is proposing countering ideologically driven violence by training local police and community members to look for signs of violent behavior.[110] According to official sources, the goal of such an effort is to incorporate tips, such as purchases of large quantities of propane, into "the day-to-day business of local police."[111] Motives, particularly religious ones, aren't always clear at the outset, so police and residents are encouraged to look out for behavior that might suggest someone is planning violent action; this approach has backing from local police, who say they are best positioned to see emerging extremism and build relationships with communities.[112] The local effort needs to be coupled with continuing and evolving intelligence and information-gathering mechanisms.

The following list of recommendations seeks to address the broader issue of indentifying, monitoring and stopping radical Islamic-inspired domestic terrorism:

- Understand the regional, country, and ethnic divisions within the Muslim-American community; first- and second-generation immigrants from certain countries (Somalia, Pakistan, Egypt, Saudi Arabia) may be more amenable and susceptible to the message of Islamic radicalization.
- Monitor the availability and download traffic of YouTube videos that are hosted by radical Islamic clerics/imams/speakers who advocate harmful acts against the American people/interests/places/targets. Encourage YouTube to remove such videos altogether through existing YouTube Community Guidelines by highlighting that the presence of these videos on the Internet serves as inspiration to individuals who seek to follow radical Islamic teachings and practices.
- Enter into direct debate in the "marketplace of ideas"—promote/support/endorse/ disseminate across the Internet the teachings/sermons/arguments of moderate Islamic clerics and scholars who argue against war/Jihad/combat with the United

---

[109] http://online.wsj.com/article/SB10001424052748703322204575226612162292130.html
[110] Ibid.
[111] Ibid.
[112] Ibid.

States and American citizens; special attention should be paid to content that refutes, discredits, and counterbalances the speeches by main Jihadist clerics on the U.S. list of international terrorists.

- Promote relationships between authorities and amateur/unofficial groups that monitor Internet traffic for terrorist, criminal, and other unlawful behavior. This type of activity helped alert authorities to Coleen LaRose's activities and led to her arrest.

- Utilize search engine optimization that promotes one type of Internet-based content over another, particularly as it applies to search for content related to radical Islamic teachings/texts/sermons/explanations of Koran/debate on Jihad/role of Muslims in non-Muslim societies.[113]

- Monitor websites/discussion boards/chat rooms that espouse radical Islamic teachings and serve as communication portals for American and foreign individuals. U.S. law enforcement and the intelligence community must go a step further and target such websites for complete removal/incapacitation from the Internet so as not to give an opportunity for men and women in the United States to absorb radical Islamic message that calls for a violent confrontation between Muslims and the Western world, particularly America.

- Recognize that passengers returning from/having evidence of being in specific countries—Pakistan, Afghanistan, Somalia—can run a higher risk of coming in contact with/having engaged with/having spent time with/having met with individuals/groups/organizations that espouse radical Islamist ideology that calls for a confrontation with/targeting of the Western world, especially the United States. Therefore, effective security technology, funded and managed through the DHS and FBI, should be utilized for the following purposes:
  - Share/train/familiarize local as well as Federal law enforcement bodies with biometric databases containing information on specific individuals.
  - Utilize electronic and surveillance-type facial recognition technology at points of entry to the United States—airports, sea ports, rail terminals, significant border crossings.

- Continue to facilitate information exchanges and establish faster linkages between the DHS, domestic intelligence agencies, and the security/community representatives at the governors' offices, the U.S. Marshals Service, chiefs of police, and attorneys general in all U.S. states and territories.

---

[113] http://en.wikipedia.org/wiki/Search_engine_optimization